Tradecraft Wisdom

From Allen Welsh Dulles

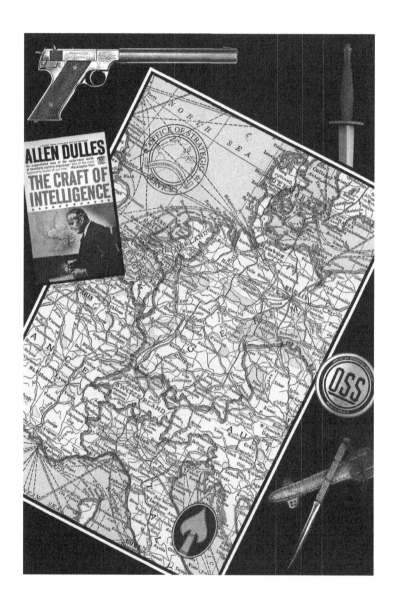

TRADECRAFT WISDOM

from Allen Welsh Dulles

JAMES LORIEGA

RAVEN
TRADECRAFT
PRESS

First Printing: January 2021

ISBN: 978-1-716-29385-6

RAVEN TRADECRAFT PRESS
Washington, DC 20505

Dedication

This small work is dedicated to all those requiring meaningful directions for living their lives—whether they recognize the need for it, or not.

Acknowledgments
My sincere gratitude to the nameless many
in Langley, VA, for their cooperation and generous access
to their collection of archival material, art, and photographs.

Disclaimer Notice

The information presented in this book is not intended to be interpreted as legal advice; nor are the descriptions of the techniques meant to take the place of proper instruction under the tutelage and supervision of a qualified and competent instructor. The techniques contained herein reflect the injurious methods used in extreme life-or-death situations. As such, they are dangerous, if not lethal, to use. They are presented here solely for informational purposes, and neither the author nor the publisher assumes any responsibility for their use.

About the Publisher

Lost Arts Publications was established in 2015 to satisfy the growing interest in unique, rare, and almost-lost martial disciplines, arts, and systems. Niche-focused on lesser-known and rarely-seen methods, from both Eastern and Western perspectives, Lost Arts Publications produces original works in both hardcover and paperback formats.

Two imprints also publish under the Lost Arts Publications banner. The *Pay-Per-Cut Press* imprint specializes in edged weapons and systems of European origin. The *Raven Tradecraft Press* imprint specializes in modern spycraft and civilian tradecraft.

The **Intelligence Tradecraft Series** is designed for the reader interested in learning elements of Tradecraft that are not widely available outside of the realm of the covert intelligence community. Given the gravity of their work, intelligence operatives in every nation have access to advanced training and instruction in the exhaustive number of physical, psychological, and social skills required of their profession. While the full complement of these unique skills is too vast to name, the teachings, tactics, and techniques they encompass are collectively known as *Tradecraft*. Simply put, they are the *crafts* of the *spy trade*.

Intelligence operatives, of course, are not the only professionals who can benefit from a knowledge of Tradecraft, and many of these skills can be similarly useful to persons who are not employed in the intelligence field. They are of great advantage to individuals involved in high-risk professions, international banking and finance, and certain echelons of corporate management. Moreover, Tradecraft competencies can benefit "regular" citizens, who are neither intelligence operatives nor work in high-risk professions, but who want to embrace some of these "spy skills" simply to be better equipped for the dangers they may encounter in their own "regular" lives.

Focused well beyond such mundane topics as personal combat, firearms, and defensive driving skills, each book in the *Intelligence Tradecraft Series* is written, illustrated, and produced to fulfill unique needs; among them, *Tradecraft for Non-Spies, Fundamental Tradecraft, Conducting Opponent Research, Acquiring Competitor Intelligence, Influencing an Adversary's Behavior, Psychological Warfare,* and similar difficult-to-find information. Each volume is written by an active or retired member of the various agencies that actively teach comparable skills to their personnel and field operatives, and the Tradecraft teachings, tactics, and techniques presented have been tried and tested by the authors or their associates.

No assertions or commentaries are made with regard to the ethics, morality, legitimacy, or justifications surrounding the practice of the subject matter. Its use is presented as a mere tool, and the manner or motives for which it is employed lie outside the scope of this primer.

—The Editors
Langley, VA

Espionage is a very serious matter for some, a deadly serious business.
It violates international law and normal codes of civilized conduct,
and yet it is virtually universal because it is considered
a matter of vital national importance to states.
Espionage generates its own rules.
—Raymond L. Garthoff
A Journey Through the Cold War

TRADECRAFT WISDOM

from Allen Welsh Dulles

Contents

FOREWORD

Few individuals outside of our intelligence community are familiar with the term *tradecraft*; and of those who know the term, few comprehend the full depth of its meaning. Some writers within the espionage genre have described tradecraft as the *tricks that spies use to gather intelligence*. Others see it as the *measures spies take to maintain their identities and activities hidden* from other spies and the public. While these and other "definitions" are accurate to some degree, none is complete.

In addition to the "tricks" of the trade and the security "measures" intelligence operatives use, tradecraft involves the *daily habits* that they must practice in *all aspects of their profession*. A lapse in adhering to tradecraft is tantamount to a lapse in personal and organizational security—and that can lead to discovery, loss of anonymity, compromise, and potentially more severe consequences.

Perhaps the principal reason why so few lay individuals fully understand the term is because tradecraft is often taught or learned *informally*, or is *acquired through experience*. In spite of those general restrictions, Mr. Loriega has through his research managed to identify a basic but functional example of "tradecraft instructions," originally assembled and authored by Allen W. Dulles.

The exceptional Mr. Dulles was the first *civilian* director of the Central Intelligence Agency. It is significant to note that he succeeded five previous Directors of Central Intelligence—or DCIs—who had been appointed to that position based on their military accomplishments, but who unfortunately lacked Dulles' unsurpassed real-world experience in covert intelligence.

Dulles, for his part, had served as Station Chief of the OFFICE OF STRATEGIC SERVICES in Bern, Switzerland during World War II. The OFFICE OF STRATEGIC SERVICES, or OSS, was established in 1941 as America's first actual intelligence agency. After having been personally recruited by OSS Director, William Donovan. Dulles and his operatives worked undetected in their Bern offices—Hitler's backyard—until the end of WWII. And ending the war was the goal which Dulles had tirelessly strategized to bring about.

The seventy-three points contained herein were *not* set down by Dulles specifically as tradecraft; he instead referred to them as "Insights on Intelligence," intending them as advice to new or veteran intelligence officers. They have been re-sequenced from their original form by Mr. Loriega, and clustered into four categories.

Times have changed and opinions run rampant regarding the role and functions of America's premiere intelligence agency; yet regardless of your familiarity (or lack of it) with Allen Dulles' place in history, or your own views of the CIA's activities, you will, I believe, find great personal value in the *de facto* "tradecraft tenets" presented here.

—J. Agriole Ames
Editor-in-Chief
Raven Tradecraft Press
Langley, VA

PREFACE

Today, as was true in the past, intelligence operatives are engaged in a profession that is profoundly dangerous on more levels than can ever be depicted in literature or cinema. The "spy melodramas" portrayed in popular fiction and films cannot begin to approximate the actual consequences that await the operative that misses a step, misses his[1] chance, or who loses his anonymity or cover.

It was in fact a strict adherence to anonymity—together with secrecy and the other tenets listed by Allen Dulles in these pages—that kept the unsung agents of the OSS safe and alive behind enemy lines during WWII. And it is those tenets that are still a requisite for modern intelligence operatives to remain safe and successful today.

Though you, the reader, may not be formally employed in the intelligence trade, you nonetheless encounter precarious situations of varying degrees in your own life. It is those precarious situations that make the sage practices assembled by DCI Dulles in this book equally relevant and applicable to you!

This volume of the *Intelligence Tradecraft Series* lists the various "rules" established by a veteran and highly-decorated intelligence officer to safeguard his operatives from making fatal but avoidable mistakes. The strategies and mindset he presents, however, are not exclusive to spies. As such, Dulles' rules can provide you with a unique set of strategies and

---

1 Please note that masculine pronouns are used throughout this book for brevity and not to disregard the presence, efforts, and sacrifices of the vast number of women who work, and have worked, in the American intelligence community.

mindset that can safeguard you from avoidable mistakes. They work for those who are exposed to danger each day of their lives. They may also work for you.

—James Loriega
New York City 2020

Part I

MICRODOT OF A LONG LIFE SPYING

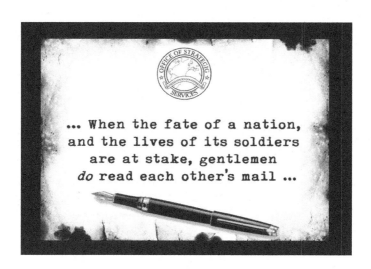

... When the fate of a nation, and the lives of its soldiers are at stake, gentlemen *do* read each other's mail ...

But first ... *who was Allen W. Dulles?*

ALLEN WELSH DULLES

Diplomat, Lawyer, Author, and Spymaster

The Preface to a multi-volume document titled ALLEN WELSH DULLES AS DIRECTOR OF CENTRAL INTELLIGENCE, completed by the CIA in early 1973 and declassified in April, 1994, begins as follows:

> *Allen Welsh Dulles was a vital, vivid man who took part personally in so many of the Agency's activities ... that an author could be overwhelmed by the task of writing about his role as Director of Central Intelligence. It is possible to emphasize the activities of Dulles during that period—what he did with his time—but such as approach would distort the record. He was fascinated by the activities of the clandestine services, particularly the political and psychological activities that are generally known as covert action.*
>
> *... He spent hours on what might be called public relations matters—talking with visitors, filling speaking engagements and corresponding with a multitude of friends. Yet he would have been the first to say that there was no necessary correlation between the hours he devoted to specific items and their importance to the Agency or his mission of making the CIA the best intelligence service in the world.*

Reading that Preface, written by Wayne G. Jackson, the reader would have no notion of Allen Dulles' incalculable intelligence contributions —first to the *Office of Strategic Services* during World War II, then to the *Central Intelligence Agency* in the Cold War era, and ultimately to this nation.

When Dwight D. Eisenhower became President in 1952, he appointed Allen Welsh Dulles as the first *civilian* Director of the Central Intelligence Agency. By that time, Dulles had already lived a full life of diplomacy, law, politics, and international intrigue—all of which began in 1916, after he graduated Princeton and entered the diplomatic service. From that point forward, Dulles enjoyed a colorful professional career; so colorful that the many books and biographies written about him make the fabricated and fictional spies of modern literature seem pale in comparison.

Early Years

Dulles was born on April 7, 1893, in Watertown, New York. After attending Princeton University, he joined the diplomatic service in 1916 and served in Vienna, Bern, Paris, Berlin and Istanbul. In 1920, he married Clover Todd. They had two daughters and one son.

Work Overseas

Initially assigned to Vienna, Dulles was transferred to Bern, Switzerland, along with the rest of the embassy personnel shortly before the U.S. entered the First World War. Later in life Dulles claimed to have been telephoned by Vladimir Lenin, seeking a meeting with the American embassy on April 8, 1917, the day before Lenin left Switzerland to travel to Saint Petersburg aboard a German train.

The following year, after recovering from the 1918 flu pandemic, Dulles was assigned to the American delegation at the Paris Peace Conference, along with his older brother, John Foster Dulles. From

1922-6, he served five years as chief of the Near East division of the Department of State.

Return to the US

Dulles returned to the United States in 1926, obtained a law degree from George Washington University Law School, and took a job at the New York City law firm of *Sullivan and Cromwell*, where his brother Foster was a partner. In 1927, Dulles became a director of the *Council on Foreign Relations*, the first new director since the Council's founding in 1921. He served as the Council's secretary from 1933 to 1944.

In 1935, Dulles returned from a business trip to Germany appalled by the Nazi treatment of German Jews. Despite his brother's objections, he led a movement within the firm of Sullivan & Cromwell to close their Berlin office. As a result of Dulles' efforts, the Berlin office was closed and the firm ceased to conduct business in Nazi Germany. Around this time, Dulles collaborated with Hamilton Fish Armstrong, the editor of *Foreign Affairs* magazine, on two books—**Can We Be Neutral?** in 1936, and **Can America Stay Neutral?** in 1939.

The Office of Strategic Services

Dulles was practicing law in 1942 when he was approached by William J. Donovan, an old friend who had been recently appointed by President Franklin D. Roosevelt as Director of the **Office of Strategic Services** (OSS) in Washinton, DC. Donovan, discussed in the next chapter, asked Dulles to head the OSS offices in New York. Soon after, in November, Dulles was transferred to Bern, Switzerland, where he served as OSS Station Chief for the duration of World War II.

OSS logo from training film

OSS Station Chief, Bern

Dulles' work in Switzerland involved collecting intelligence regarding German plans and activities, and establishing wide contacts with German émigrés, resistance fighters, and anti-Nazi intelligence officers. Among the best-document activities as Bern Station Chief was Dulles' connection with Operation Valkyrie—the 1944 German plot to assassinate Hitler, whicht failed only by the "sheerest of accidents."

Allen Dulles

Dulles also received valuable information from Fritz Kolbe, a German diplomat whom he described as the best spy of the war. Kolbe supplied secret documents relating to active German spies and plans for the Messerschmitt Me 262 jet fighter. In 1945 Dulles was a key player in *Operation Sunrise*, conducting secret negotiatiations with German commanders in Italy which ultimately led to their surrender.

The Central Intelligence Agency

After the war, President Harry S. Truman ordered the Office of Strategic Services to be closed down in October 1945 and its functions transferred to the State and War Departments. However, two years later the disbanded OSS' structure provided a model for the **Central Intelligence Agency** (CIA) that was established in September 1947.

In 1948 Dulles was made chairman of a three-man committee charged with surveying the U.S. intelligence system. In 1949 they co-authored the *Dulles–Jackson–Correa Report*, which was sharply critical of the newly-established CIA. Partly as a result of the report, President Truman named a new Director of Central Intelligence, Lieutenant General Walter Bedell Smith. Director Smith, in turn, recruited Dulles to oversee the agency's covert operations as Deputy Director for Plans, a position accepted on January 4, 1951.

On August 23, 1951, Dulles was promoted to Deputy Director of Central Intelligence, making him second in the intelligence hierarchy. After the election of Dwight Eisenhower to President in 1952, Bedell Smith shifted to the Department of State and Dulles became the first civilian Director of Central Intelligence.

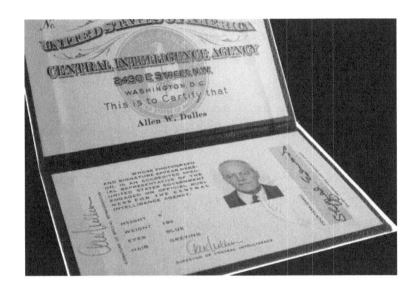

Dulles ran the CIA as he had his OSS station in Switzerland. He believed that intelligence was a key part of American foreign policy and that the network of associations, the breadth of vision, and the daring he had displayed fighting the Nazis would succeed in battling communism.

Spying during the war and afterwards was a gentleman's pursuit, he believed, practiced in the shadows by and among "men of affairs" like him, who were comfortable bending ethics or cutting legal corners for a higher cause. Though he talked little about Donovan after the war, Dulles's operating style mirrored the general's in many ways. Like Donovan, Dulles showed no interest in managing the CIA's inner workings, leaving them to his deputies so he could be free to dabble in the clandestine operations that interested him.

In 1953, Dulles was involved in a covert operation that led to the removal of democratically elected prime minister of Iran, Mohammad Mossadegh, and his replacement with Mohammad Reza Pahlavi, Shah of Iran. In 1954, President Jacobo Arbenz Guzman of Guatemala was removed in a CIA-led coup carried out under the code name Operation PBSUCCESS. The Agency also succeeded in obtaining a copy of Nikita Khrushchev's secret speech of 1956 denouncing Joseph Stalin.

Bay of Pigs

Several failed assassination plots utilizing CIA-recruited operatives and anti-Castro Cubans directly against Castro undermined the CIA's credibility. The reputation of the agency and its director declined drastically after the *Bay of Pigs Invasion* fiasco. President Kennedy reportedly said he wanted to "*splinter the CIA into a thousand pieces and scatter it into the winds.*" However, following a "*rigorous inquiry into the agency's affairs, methods, and problems ... [Kennedy] did not 'splinter' it after all and did not recommend Congressional supervision.*"

It was, however, during this period that Dulles faced increasing criticism. In autumn 1961, following the Bay of Pigs incident and Algiers plot to overthrow Charles de Gaulle, Dulles and his entourage

—which included Deputy Director for Plans Richard M. Bissell Jr. and Deputy Director Charles Cabell—were forced to resign. On November 28, 1961, Kennedy presented Dulles with the National Security Medal at the CIA Headquarters in Langley, Virginia. The next day, November 29, the White House released a resignation letter signed by Dulles.

Legacy

Dulles is considered one of the essential creators of the modern United States intelligence system and was an indispensable guide to clandestine operations during the Cold War. He established intelligence networks worldwide to check and counter Soviet and eastern European communist advances as well as international communist movements.

In 1963 Dulles published the book, **The Craft of Intelligence**, and in 1968 he edited **Great True Spy Stories**, which included accounts of his own acrivities in the Second World War. He died on January 29, 1969, of influenza, complicated by pneumonia, at the age of 75, in Georgetown, D.C. He was buried in Green Mount Cemetery in Baltimore, Maryland.

A LIFE IN INTELLIGENCE

To better appreciate the insights DCI Allen Dulles set down for clandestine operatives, it will be helpful to understand the stakes involved in American intelligence activities within the context of World War II and Cold War eras.

Reading Other People's Mail

Historically, Americans have harbored an ambivalence—if not an outright *dislike*—for espionage. This is true despite the fact that covert intelligence activities played a vital role in our history, even before the nation earned its independence. In fact, Washington was using scouts and spies from the moment he took command of the Continental Army in 1775. It is perhaps a national sense of cognitive dissonance that hypocritically allows us to enjoy television spy dramas like *The Americans* or *Turn* while claiming to detest the notion of spying.

Shutting Down Intelligence Collection

In 1929, when Secretary of State Henry Stimson was provided with deciphered Japanese diplomatic messages, he is quoted as saying. *"Gentlemen do not read each other's mail"* before shutting down the State Department's cryptography office in charge of cracking Japanese codes. It was in fact Allen Dulles who, years later—after serving as both as an OSS station chief and as CIA Director—succinctly clarified the need for intelligence. *"When the fate of a nation and the lives of its soldiers are at stake,"* he offered, *"gentlemen do read each other's mail."*

Our Lack of Centralized Intelligence

But in the pre-WWII era, most Americans were oblivious to what was happening in Europe. In July, 1939, Senator William E. Borah (an isolationist-minded Senator from Iowa) opined, *"There is not going to be any war in Europe. At least not soon. Germany is not ready for it. All this [war] hysteria is manufactured and artificial."* It was a mere six weeks later, on September 1, 1939, that the German military invaded Poland. Two days after that, Britain and France declared war on Germany. And still at that time, America's own capacity for centralized intelligence was nonexistent. Fortunately, cooler heads were starting to prevail.

When the fate of a nation and the lives of its soldiers are at stake, *gentlemen do read each other's mail.*

It's time to fight like our enemies

As our entry into WWII grew imminent, President Roosevelt became aware of the dire need to collect, collate, and analyze the sporadic information being gathered from no less than four disparate sources: 1) the State Department, 2) the War Office[2], 3) the Office of Naval Intelligence, and 4) the FBI's own *Special Intelligence Service*.

In July, 1941, he created the Office of the *Coordinator of Information* (COI), a civilian office responsible for collating intelligence information and reporting significant discoveries. **William Donovan** was appointed as the COI director. Donovan, an energetic visionary nicknamed "Wild Bill" by those who knew him, was a tough and smart veteran of World War I who received the Medal of Honor for heroism.

"Wild Bill" Donovan—America's First Modern Spymaster

Both the Navy and the Army had access to various Japanese coded messages; yet their refusal to share information and work together was

---

2 Which oversaw the US Army's *Military Intelligence Division*

a major reason why the Japanese achieved surprise and destroyed much of the Pacific fleet in Pearl Harbor. The attack forced an *unprepared* United States into World War II, and our failure to prevent it became one of the driving forces for more and better strategic intelligence.

Some months following the attack on Pearl Harbor, the COI became the Office of Strategic Services. Donovan, who had spent some time in Great Britain studying their **Special Operations Executive** (SOE)—the department set up by the government in 1940—stayed on as the first director of the OSS. Donovan's understanding of the SOE, and his contacts there, would serve as a model for America's OSS.

Ph.D's Who Can Win a Bar Fight

Agents were recruited for skills rather than background. A battery of mental and physical tests was followed by personality assessments that identified a candidate's intelligence, imagination, creativity, courage, and ruthlessness. An ideal candidate was deemed to be a "*Ph.D. who can win a bar fight.*"

Many of the first members of OSS were Donovan's friends and colleagues. These included various well-to-do New York lawyers and socialites, one of whom was Allen Dulles. But the OSS was not merely a group of gentlemen spies. There were also talented individuals from many walks of life, such as film director John Ford, Boston White Sox ball player *Moe Berg*, Jazz age icon *Josephine Baker*, and *Julia* Child.

The Depth of OSS Training

Winning the *War of Wits*

The OSS grew quickly, taking on responsibilities for espionage and unconventional warfare in addition to research and analysis. New recruits were taught the use of small arms, but knew that to survive in enemy territory, their reliance on weapons had to be *minimal*. They were outfitted with creative accessories, like small concealable "*lapel daggers*" in their clothes, *scarves with maps* printed to their design, and many other covert items.

Close-quarter combat consisted of a method of fighting that combined the Chinese martial arts with Japanese jujutsu and basic street brawling. Initially called "Gutter-fighting," it was later given the more respectable name of *The Fairbairn Protocol* after its creator, William E. Fairbairn. The essence of training was doing *whatever* was necessary to survive in the "War of Wits," as espionage was generally called.

Disbanding the OSS

When the US entered WWII, Americans were relatively new to centralized espionage, and many had been skeptical of Donovan's agency and ideas. The greatest successes of the OSS came not from glamorous acts of daring but from the painstaking and carefully planned work of professionals. Yet, after securing Allied victory, President Truman disbanded the OSS on September 20, 1945. Six days after Truman shut down the OSS, Assistant Secretary of War John McCloy created the military's *Strategic Services Unit*, stating, "... *the continuing operations of OSS must be performed in order to preserve them.*"

CIA—the New OSS

In light of the pervasive Soviet threat, Truman eventually corrected his error, and the National Security Act of 1947 established the **Central Intelligence Agency**. Ultimately, the Act created the very same permanent, global intelligence network that Donovan and Dulles had envisioned for the OSS.

Spying was a gentleman's pursuit,
practiced in the shadows by and among "men of affairs" like himself

Part II

LIFE LESSONS FROM THE SHADOWS

Be all things to all men, but *don't* betray your principles. It is your job to bend circumstances to your will, not to let them bend or twist you ...

Be all things to all, but don't betray your principles ...

On Personal Traits

The greatest weapon a man or woman can bring to this type of work in which we are engaged is his or her hard common sense. The following notes aim at being a little common sense and applied form. Simple common sense crystallized by a certain amount of experience into a number of rules and suggestions.

—Allen W. Dulles

- **Easiness and confidence** do not come readily to all of us. *They must be assiduously cultivated.* Not only because they help us personally, but they also help to produce similar reactions in those we are handling.

- **Always be polite to people,** but not exaggeratedly so. With the following class of persons who come to know you—hotel and restaurant staffs, taxi drivers, train personnel etc., be pleasant. Someday, they may prove useful to you. Be generous in your tips to them, but again, not exaggeratedly so. Give just a little more than the other fellow does—unless the cover under which you are working does not permit this. Give only normal tips, however, to waiters and taxi drivers, etc., when you are on the job. Don't give them any stimulus, even of gratification, to make you stick in their minds. Be as brief and casual as possible.

- When you think a man is possessed of useful knowledge or may in other ways be of value to you, **remember that praise is acceptable to the vast majority of men**. When honest praise is difficult, a spot of flattery will do equally well.

- **Never deal out the intense, the dramatic stuff**, to a person before you have quietly obtained his confidence in your levelheadedness.

- **Gain the confidence of your agents**, but be wary of giving them more of yours than is necessary. He may fall by the way side; he may quarrel with you; it may be advisable for a number of reasons to drop him. In that case, obviously, the less information he possesses, the better. Equally obviously, if an agent runs the risk of falling into the hands of the enemy, it is unfair both to him and the show to put him in possession of more knowledge than he needs.

- **Do not be afraid to be harsh**, or even harsh with others, if it is your duty to be so. You are expected to be likewise with yourself. When necessity arises neither your own feelings nor those of others matter. Only the job—the lives and safety of those entrusted to you—is what counts.

- **Become a real friend of your agents.** Remember that he has a human side so bind him to you by taking an interest in his personal affairs and in his family. But never let the friendship be stronger than your sense of duty to the work. That must always be impervious to any sentimental considerations. Otherwise, your vision will be distorted, your judgment affected, and you may be reluctant, even, to place your men in a position of danger. You may also, by indulgence toward him, let him endanger others.

- **Remember that you have no right to expect of others what you are not prepared to do yourself.** But on the other hand, do not rashly expose yourself in any unnecessary displays of personal courage that may endanger the whole shooting match. It often takes more moral courage to ask another fellow to do a dangerous task than to do it yourself. But if this is the proper course to follow, then you must follow it.

- Within the limits of your principles, **be all things to all men. But don't betray your principles**. The strongest force in your show is you. Your sense of right, your sense of respect for yourself and others. And it is your job to bend circumstances to your will, not to let circumstances bend or twist you.

- Away from the job, among your other contacts, **never know too much.** Often you will have to bite down on your vanity, which would like to show what you know. This is especially hard when you hear a wrong assertion being made or a misstatement of events.

- **Not knowing too much does not mean not knowing anything**. Unless there is a special reason for it, it is not good either to appear a nitwit or a person lacking in discretion. This does not invite the placing of confidence in you.

- **Show your intelligence, but be quiet on anything along the line you are working.** Make others do the speaking. A good thing sometimes is to be personally interested as "a good patriot and anxious to pass along anything useful to official channels in the hope that it may eventually get to the right quarter."

- **If anything, overestimate the opposition**. Certainly never underestimate it. But do not let that lead to nervousness or lack of confidence. Don't get rattled, and know that with hard work, calmness, and by never irrevocably compromising yourself, you can always, always best them.

- **Booze is naturally dangerous.** *So also is an undisciplined attraction for the other sex.* The first loosens the tongue. The second does likewise. It also distorts vision and promotes indolence. They both provide grand weapons to an enemy.

- It has been proved time and again, in particular, that **sex and business do not mix.**

Booze is naturally dangerous. So also is an undisciplined attraction for the other sex. *They both provide grand weapons to an enemy.*

- **Never get into a rut.** Or rest on your oars. There are always new lines around the corner, always changes and variations to be introduced. Unchanging habits of work lead to carelessness and detection.

- In your work, **always be in harmony with your own conscience.** Put yourself periodically in the dock for cross examination. You can never do more than your best; *only your best is good enough*. And remember that only the job counts— not you personally, excepting satisfaction of a job well done.

- It is one of the finest jobs going, no matter how small the part you play may appear to be. Countless people would give anything to be in it. Remember that and appreciate the privilege. No matter what others may do, **play your part well**.

ON THE INTELLIGENCE PROFESSION

In the fifth century B.C. the Chinese sage Sun Tzu wrote that foreknowledge was "the reason the enlightened prince and the wise general conquer the enemy whenever they move."

In 1955, the task force on Intelligence Activities of the second Herbert Hoover Commission in its advisory report to the government stated that "Intelligence deals with all the things which should be known in advance of initiating a course of action."

Both statements, widely separated as they are in time, have in common the emphasis on the practical use of advance information in its relation to action.

—Allen W. Dulles

- **In this job, there are no hours**. That is to say, one never leaves it down. It is lived. One never drops one's guard. All locations are good for laying a false trail (social occasions, for instance, a casual hint here, a phrase there). All locations are good for picking something up, or collecting ... for making a useful acquaintance.

- In a more normal sense of the term "no hours," it is certainly not a business **where people put their own private arrangements before their work**.

- **That is not to say that one does not take recreation and holidays**. Without them it is not possible to do a decent job. If there is a real goodwill and enthusiasm for the work, the two

43

(except in abnormal circumstances) will always be combined without the work having to suffer.

- **Do not overwork your cover** to the detriment of your jobs; we must never get so engrossed in the latter as to forget the former.

ON TRADECRAFT

The essence of espionage is access. Someone, or some device, has to get close enough to a thing, a place, or a person to observe or discover the desired facts without arousing the attention of those who protect them.

The information must then be delivered to the people who want it. It must move quickly or it may get "stale." And it must not get lost or be intercepted en route.

—Allen W. Dulles

- **The cover you choose will depend upon the type of work that you have to do.** So also will the social life in which you indulge. It may be necessary to lead a full social existence; it may be advisable to stay in the background. *You must school yourself not to do any wishful thinking in the sense of persuading yourself that what you want to do is what you ought to do.*

- Your cover and social behavior, naturally, ought to be chosen to fit in with your background and character. Neither should be too much of a strain. Use them well. **Imprint them, gradually but steadfastly on people's minds.** When your name crops up in conversation they must have something to say about you, something concrete outside of your real work.

- The place you live in is often a thorny problem. Hotels are seldom satisfactory. **A flat of your own where you have**

everything under control is desirable; if you can share it with a discreet friend who is not in the business, so much the better. You can relax into a normal life when you get home, and he will also give you an opportunity of cover.

Obviously **the greatest care is to be taken in the choice of servants**. But it is preferable to have a reliable servant than to have none at all. People cannot get in to search or fix telephones, etc. in your absence. And if you want to not be at home for awkward callers (either personal or telephonic), servants make that possible.

- If a man is married, the presence of his wife may be an advantage or disadvantage. That will depend on the nature of the job—**as well as on the nature of the husband and wife**.

- Should a husband tell his wife what he is doing? It is taken for granted that people in this line are possessed of discretion and judgment. If a man thinks his wife is to be trusted, then he may certainly tell her what he is doing—without necessarily telling her the confidential details of particular jobs. It would be fair to neither husband nor wife to keep her in the dark unless there were serious reasons demanding this. **A wife would naturally have to be coached in behavior in the same way as an agent.**

- **Never leave things lying about unattended** or lay them down where you are liable to forget them. Learn to write lightly; the "blank" page underneath has often been read. Be wary of your piece of blotting paper. If you have to destroy a document, do so thoroughly.

Carry as little written matter as possible, and for the shortest possible time. Never carry names or addresses *en clair*. If you cannot carry them for the time being *in your head*, put them in a species of *personal code, which only you understand*. Small papers and envelopes or cards and photographs, ought to be clipped on to the latter, otherwise they are liable to get lost. But **when you have conducted an interview or made arrangements for a meeting, write it all down and put it safely away** for reference. Your memory can play tricks.

In this job, there are no hours ...

- **The greatest vice in the game is that of carelessness.** Mistakes made generally cannot be rectified.

- **The next greatest vice is that of vanity.** Its offshoots are multiple and malignant.

- Besides, **the man with a swelled head never learns.** And *there is always a great deal to be learned*.

- Even though you feel the curious outsider has probably a good idea that you are not what you purport to be, never admit it. Keep on playing the other part. **It's amazing how often people will be led to think they were mistaken.** Or at least that you are out 'in the other stuff' only in a very mild way. And anyhow, a person is quite free to think what he likes. The important thing is that neither by admission or implication do you let him know.

- **The greatest material curse to the profession, despite all its advantages, is undoubtedly the telephone.** It is a constant source of temptation to slackness. And even if you do not use it carelessly yourself, the other fellow, very often will, so in any case, warn him. Always act on the principle that every conversation is listened to, that a call may always give the enemy a line. Naturally, always unplug during confidential conversations. Even better is it to have no phone in your room, or else have it in a box or cupboard.

The phone—capable of eavesdropping on or tracking us, and the greatest material curse to the profession

- Sometimes, for quite exceptional reasons, it may be permissible to use open post as a channel of communications. **Without these quite exceptional reasons,** allowing of no alternative, **it is to be completely avoided.**

- When the post is used, it will be advisable to get through post boxes; that is to say, people who will receive mail for you and pass it on. **This ought to be their only function.** They should not be part of the show. They will have to be chosen for the personal friendship which they have with you or with one of your agents. The explanation you give them will depend on circumstances; the letters, of course, must be apparently innocent in content. A *phrase, signature* or embodied code will give the message. **The letter ought to be concocted in such fashion as to fit in with the recipient's social background.** The writer ought therefore to be given details of the post boxes assigned to them.

The letter ought to be concocted in such fashion as to fit in with the recipient's social background.

An insipid letter is in itself suspicious. If however, a signature or phrase is sufficient to convey the message, then a card with greetings will do.

- **Make a day's journey, rather than take a risk,** either by phone or post. If you do not have a prearranged message to give by phone, never dial your number before having thought about your conversation. Do not improvise even the dummy part of it. But do not be too elaborate. The great rule here, as in all else connected with the job, is to be natural.

- If you have phoned a line or a prospective line of yours from a public box and have to look up the number, **do not leave the book lying open on that page**[3].

- When you choose a safe house to use for meetings or as a depo**t, let it be *safe*.** If you can, avoid one that is overlooked by other houses. If it is, the main entrance should be that used for other houses as well. Make sure there are no suspicious servants. Especially, of course, **be sure of the occupants**. Again, these should be chosen for reasons of personal friendship with some member of the organization and should be discreet. The story told to them will once again depend on circumstances. They should have no other place in the show, or if this is unavoidable, then calls at the house should be made as far as possible after dark.

- **Always be yourself.** Always be natural inside the setting you have cast for yourself. This is especially important when meeting people for the first time or when traveling on a job or when in restaurants or public places in the course of one. In trains or restaurants people have ample time to study those nearest them. **The calm quiet person attracts little attention.** Never strain after an effect. You would not do so in ordinary life. Look upon your job as perfectly normal and natural.

---

3 This important but dated advice relates to the use of *Yellow Pages* and phone directories. The advice remains highly relevant, however, as pertains to the modern version of the Yellow Pages—*the Internet search*. Erase your browsing history and cover your tracks.

**The greatest vice in the game is that of *carelessness*.
Mistakes made generally cannot be rectified.**

- When involved in business, *look at other people as little as possible,* and don't dawdle. You will then have a good chance of passing unnoticed. **Looks draw looks.**

- **Do not dress in a fashion calculated to strike the eye** or to single you out easily.

- Do not stand around. And as well as being punctual yourself, **see that those with whom you are dealing are punctual.** Especially if the meeting is in a public place; a man waiting around will draw attention. But even if it is not in a public place, try to arrive and make others arrive on the dot. *An* *arrival before the time causes as much inconvenience as one after time.*

- If you have a rendezvous, first **make sure you are not followed. Tell the other person to do likewise.** But do not act in any exaggerated fashion. Do not take a taxi to a house address connected with your work. If it cannot be avoided, make sure you are not under observation when you get into it. Or give another address, such as that of a café or restaurant nearby.

If you have a rendezvous, *first make sure you are not followed.*

- Try to **avoid journeys to places where you will be noticeable**. If you have to make such journeys, repeat them as little as possible, and take all means to make yourself fit in quietly with the background.

- **Make as many of your difficult appointments as you can after dark.** Turn the blackout to good use. If you cannot make it after dark, **make it very early morning when people are only half awake** and not on the lookout for strange goings-on.

- **Avoid restaurants, cafes and bars** for meetings and conversations. Above all never make an initial contact in one of them. Let it be outside. Use abundance of detail and description of persons to be met, and have one or two good distinguishing marks. have a password that can be given to the wrong person without unduly exciting infestation.

- If interviews cannot be conducted in a safe house, **then take a walk together in the country.** Cemeteries, museums and churches are useful places to bear in mind.

- Use your own judgment as to **whether or not you ought to talk to chance travel or table companions.** It may be useful. It may be the opposite. It may be of no consequence whatsoever. Think, however, before you enter upon a real conversation, whether this particular enlargement of the number of those who will recognize and spot you in the future is liable or not to be a disadvantage. **Always carry reading matter.** Not only will it save you from being bored, it is protective armor if you want to avoid a conversation or to break off an embarrassing one.

If interviews cannot be conducted in a safe house, *take a walk in the country*

- If you're angling for a man, **lead him around to where you want him; put the obvious idea in his head,** and make the suggestion of possibilities come to him. Express, if necessary - but with great tact—a wistful disbelief in the possibilities at which you are aiming. *"How fine it would be if only someone could... but of course, etc. etc."* And **always leave a line of retreat open to yourself.**

- **Never take a person for granted.** Very seldom judge a person to be above suspicion. Remember that **we live by deceiving others. Others live by deceiving us.** Unless others take persons for granted or believe in them, we would never get our results. The others have people as clever as we; if they can be taken in, so can we. Therefore, be suspicious.

- **Above all, *don't deceive yourself.*** Don't decide that the other person is fit or is all right, because you yourself would like it to be that way. You are dealing in people's lives.

- When you have made a contact, **till you are absolutely sure of your man**—and perhaps even then—**be a small but eager intermediary**. Have a "They" in the background for whom you act and to whom you are responsible. If "They" are harsh, if "They" decide to break it off, **it is never any fault of yours**, and indeed **you can pretend to have a personal grievance about it**. "They" are always great gluttons for results and very stingy with cash until "They" get them. When the results come along, "They" always send messages of congratulation and encouragement.

- Try to **find agents who do not work for money alone,** but for conviction. Remember, however, that not by conviction alone, does the man live. If they need financial help, give it to them. And avoid the "woolly" type of idealist, the fellow who lives in the clouds.

- If your agent can be laid off work periodically, this is a very good thing. And during his rest periods, **let him show himself in another field and in other capacities.**

- **Teach them at least the elements of technique.** Do not merely leave it to his own good judgment, and then hope for the best. Insist, for a long time at least, on his not showing too much initiative, but make him carry out strictly the instructions which you give him. His initiative will he tested when unexpected circumstances arise. **Tell him off soundly when he errs; praise him when he does well.**

- But if your agent knows the ground on which he is working better than you, **always be ready to listen to his advice and to consult him**. The man on the spot is the man who can judge.

- In the same way, if you get directives from HQ which to you seem ill-advised, **do not be afraid to oppose these directives.** You are there for pointing things out. This is particularly so if there is grave danger to security without a real corresponding advantage for which the risk may be taken. For that, fight anybody with everything you've got.

- **If you have several groups, keep them separate** unless the moment comes for concerted action. Keep your lines separate; and within the bounds of reason and security, try to multiply them. Each separation and each multiplication minimizes the danger of total loss. Multiplication of lines also gives the possibility of resting each line, which is often a very desirable thing.

- **Never set a thing really going,** whether it be big or small, **before you see it in its details.** Do not count on luck. Or only on bad luck.

- When using couriers, who are in themselves trustworthy (here again, the important element of personal friendship ought to be made to play its part) but whom it is better to keep in the dark as to the real nature of what they are carrying, **commercial smuggling will often provide an excellent cover**. Apart from being a valid reason for secrecy, it gives people a kick and also provides one with a reason for offering payment. Furthermore, **it involves a courier in something in which it is in his own personal advantage to conceal.**

- To build this cover, should there be no bulk of material to pass, but only a document or a letter, it will be well always to **enclose this properly sealed in a field dummy parcel** with an unsealed outer wrapping

- The ingredients for any new setup are: serious consideration of the field and of the elements at your disposal; the finding of one key man or more; safe surroundings for encounter; safe houses to meet in; post boxes; couriers; the finding of natural covers and pretext for journeys, etc.; the division of labor; separation into cells; the principal danger in constructing personal friendships between the elements (this is enormously important); avoidance of repetition.

- **The thing to aim at**, unless it is a question of a special job, **is not quick results**, which may blow up the show, **but the initiation of a series of results**, which will keep on growing and which, because the show has the proper protective mechanism to keep it under cover, will lead to discovery.

- **Serious groundwork is much more important than rapid action**. The organization does not merely consist of the people actively working but the potential agents whom you have placed where they may be needed, and upon whom you may call, if need arises.

- As with an organization, so with a particular individual. **His first job in a new field is to forget about everything excepting his groundwork**; that is, **the effecting of his cover**. *Once people label him, the job is half done.* People take things so much for granted and *only with difficulty change their sizing-up of a man once they have made it.* They have to be jolted out of it. It is up to you to see that they are not. If they do suspect, do not take it that all is lost and accept the position. **Go back to your cover and build it up again.** You will at first puzzle them, and finally persuade them.

SECURITY

There are many virtues to be striven after in the job. The greatest of them all is security. All else must be subordinated to that....

61

SECURITY

- There are many virtues to be striven after in the job. **The greatest of them all is security**. All else must be subordinated to that.

- Security consists not only in avoiding big risks. **It consists in carrying out daily tasks with painstaking remembrance of the tiny things that security demands.** *The little things are in many ways more important than the big ones. It is they which oftenest give the game away.* It is consistent care in them, which form the habit and characteristic of security mindedness.

- In any case, **the man or woman who does not indulge in the daily security routine**, boring and useless though it may sometimes appear, **will be found lacking in the proper instinctive reaction** when dealing with the bigger stuff.

- No matter how brilliantly given an individual, no matter how great his good will, **if he is lacking in security, he will eventually prove more of a liability than asset.**

The man or woman who does not indulge in the daily security routine, boring though it may sometimes appear, **will be found lacking**

- Security, of course, does not mean stagnation or being afraid to go after things. **It means going after things, but reducing all the risks** to a minimum by hard work.

- Lastly, and above all, *remember security*.

The above points are not intended for any cursory, even interested, glance. They will bear—each of them—serious attention, and at least occasional re-perusal.

It is probable, furthermore, that dotted here and there among them will be found claims that have particular present application for each person who reads them. These, naturally, are meant to be acted upon straightaway.

—Allen W. Dulles

ABOUT THE EDITOR

In 1984, James Loriega founded the New York Ninpokai, a training facility which soon came to be regarded as "the premier academy for the traditional ninjutsu in NYC." Loriega began his formal martial arts training in 1967 with the late Grandmaster Ronald Duncan, the first non-Japanese to teach the ninja arts in the United States—and the acknowledged *Father of American Ninjutsu*. Though he later trained with other Japanese ninjutsu masters, it was from Duncan-sensei that Loriega learned the myriad strategies, tactics, and disciplines that comprise ninjutsu.

During the mid-80s, he began writing extensively around that same time, and from 1985 to 1995 served as Technical Consultant and Contributing Editor for **Ninja** magazine, an international publication dedicated exclusively to ninjutsu. His overseas travels to teach ninjutsu also exposed Loriega to the western martial arts of Europe and the Mediterranean, and his subsequent training in those arts led to instructor ranks in other disciplines.

In January of 2002, Loriega was recognized as a master in western arts by the *International Masters-at-Arms Federation* (IMAF), based in Milan, Italy. The IMAF, now dissolved, was an organization of professional instructors of Historical and Classical edged weapons. In February of 2018, he was recognized by the *Martial Arts University*'s President, Michael DePasquale, as a *Martial Arts Icon*—an individual who is symbolic of an idea and leaves a memorable mark on the lives of those he teaches. In April of 2018, he was recognized as a *Ninjutsu Scholar* and inducted by President Dan McEaddy into the *International Circle of Masters* (ICM).

Loriega holds instructor ranks in Ninjutsu, Jujutsu, and Aikijujutsu, as well as in a number of Western martial arts. He has published over two dozen books on tradecraft, martial arts, and civilian defensive tactics, and his extensive writings have appeared in mainstream martial arts publications such as *Soldier of Fortune*, *Black Belt*, *Inside Kung-Fu, Tactical Knives*, and *Ninja* magazines.

INTELLIGENCE TRADECRAFT SERIES

TRADECRAFT

Book I
Fundamentals

A Reference Book for Intel Ops
A Manual for the Rest of Us

James Loriega

INTELLIGENCE TRADECRAFT SERIES

KNOW YOUR ENEMY
Conducting Opposition Research

J. Agriole Ames

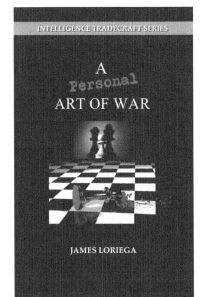

INTELLIGENCE TRADECRAFT SERIES

A
Personal
ART OF WAR

JAMES LORIEGA

INTELLIGENCE TRADECRAFT SERIES

Fundamentals of
**COMPETITOR
INTELLIGENCE**

J. Agriole Ames

Other Tradecraft titles in this series

BIBLIOGRAPHY

Dulles, Allen. **The Craft of Intelligence**. New York: Harper & Row, 1963.

— **True Great Spy Stories**. Los Angeles, CA: Castle Publications, Ltd. 1984

— **Germany's Underground**. Boston, MA: Da Capo Press. 2000

— **The Secret Surrender**. Lanham, MD: Lyons Press. 2006

Fairbairn, William E. **Get Tough**. Boulder, CO: Paladin Press. 1943

FitzMaurice, Eugene. **The Hawkeland Cache**. New York: Wyndham Books (Simon & Schuster.) 1980

Grose, Peter. **Gentleman Spy**: *The Life of Allen Dulles*. MA: Unv of Massachusetts Press. 1996.

Korda, Michael. **Power**: *How to Get It; How to Use It*. New York: Random House. 1975

LeCarré, John. **Tinker, Tailor, Soldier, Spy**. New York: Alfred A. Knopf. 1974

Loriega, James. **Ninjutsu in the Articles of Sun Tzu**. New York: Lost Arts Publications. 2018

— **Ninjutsu in the Sayings of Wu Tzu**. New York: Lost Arts Publications. 2018

— **Basic Principles of Psychological Operations**. Washington, DC: Raven Tradecraft Press. 2018

— **Know Your Enemy**: *Conducting Opponent Research*. Washington, DC: Raven Tradecraft Press. 2018

— **Dressed to Kill**. Washington, DC: Raven Tradecraft Press. 2019

— **The OSS Combat Manual**. Washington, DC: Raven Tradecraft Press. 2019

Mendez, Antonio J. **Master of Disguise**: *My Secret Life in th CIA*. New York: William Morrow. 1999

— **The Moscow Rules**. New York: Public Affairs. 2019

Miller, Scott. **Agent 110**: *An American Spymaster and the German Resistance in WWII*. New York: Simon & Schuster. 2017

Waller, Douglas. **Wild Bill Donovan**: *The Spymaster Who Created the OSS and Modern American Espionage.* (2011)

—   **Disciples**: *The World War II Missions of the CIA Directors Who Fought for Wild Bill Donovan.* New York: Simon & Schuster. 2015

Srodes, James. **Allen Dulles**: *Master of Spies.* Washington, DC: Regnery History. 2000

Sun Tzu. **The Art of War**. Trans. Samuel Griffith. London: Oxford University Press, 1963

Talbot, David. **The Devil's Chessboard**. New York: Harper Perennial. 2016

Made in the USA
Las Vegas, NV
01 March 2023

68328757R00039